Wales

Books by W. A. Poucher
available from Constable

Scotland
The magic of Skye
The Scottish Peaks
The Peak and Pennines
The Lakeland Peaks
The Welsh Peaks

Other books now out of print

The backbone of England
Climbing with a camera
Escape to the hills
A camera in the Cairngorms
Scotland through the lens
Highland holiday
The North Western Highlands
Lakeland scrapbook
Lakeland through the lens
Lakeland holiday
Lakeland journey
Over lakeland fells
Wanderings in Wales
Snowdonia through the lens
Snowdon holiday
Peak panorama
The Surrey hills
The magic of the Dolomites
West country journey
Journey into Ireland

Yr Aran from Llyn Gwynant

(frontispiece)

Cradled in its beautiful setting, this lake lies in Nantgwynant, which stretches southwards from Pen-y-Gwryd to Beddgelert. Its many moods charm the eye of the passing visitor, and its shores disclose the finest view of Yr Aran, a satellite of Snowdon.

WALES
W.A.Poucher

Book Club Associates
London

This edition published 1981 by
Book Club Associates
By arrangement with Constable & Co Ltd
Copyright © 1981 by W.A. Poucher
Filmset by Servis Filmsetting Ltd, Manchester
Printed and bound in Japan by
Dai Nippon Company, Tokyo

The photographs

Preface

Wales has been my happy hunting-ground for the past forty years and I have enjoyed every moment spent in discovering the magnificence of its landscape, and in talking to its people. It is largely a land of mountains, rimmed by an attractive cliff-lined coast, and dominated by the grandeur of Snowdon, the highest peak south of the Border; by the splendour of Cadair Idris, a great mountain in central Wales; and by the picturesque Brecon Beacons in the south, as well as the relatively unknown Carmarthen Fan. In photographing this fine scenery I used Kodachrome and monochrome with my two Leicas and a Leicaflex, together with a variety of lenses.

I have written and illustrated in monochrome some thirty books portraying the magnificent scenery to be found by walking Britain's dales and climbing its hills, but this is only my second book in colour; and I hope it will not only please my many Welsh friends, but also the thousands of readers of my other Pictorial Guides which cover Scotland, Skye, the Lake District, the Peak District and the Pennines. Readers of this book who are interested in mountain walking and climbing will find a complete account in my *Welsh Peaks* of the safe ascent of the hills pictured herein.

To anyone who knows Wales, the plan I have adopted for this book will be obvious; but for those who are not so fortunate and wish to see for themselves the best of Welsh scenery from a car, this will be an indispensable guide, for one scene follows another in the order of their appearance from south to north. Moreover, it will be clear that my greatest interest as a mountain photographer is in the portrayal of nature's masterpieces, rather than in the works of man; although in a few pictures, such as those of Caernarfon and Beddgelert which have a special appeal, I have included them for this specific reason.

W. A. Poucher
4, Heathfield
Reigate Heath
Surrey
1981

Lydstep Caverns

Sprinkle Haven is within easy reach of Tenby, and the spectacular rocky façade of Lydstep Caverns makes a splendid prelude to the fine cliff scenery of the Pembrokeshire coast, stretching away to the west where the view of Saddle Head from the Stack Rocks is perhaps the most magnificent scene of them all.

But the beautiful coast of the Gower Peninsula should not be overlooked because it includes Three Cliffs Bay – a small inlet of the vast sweep of Oxwich Bay – which is unique. Two isolated cliffs jut skywards from the sea: the first is the Great Tor, a pinnacled mass of limestone, and the second is Benwick. Both will attract the passing climber. Their finest elevation is revealed from the sea, but at low tide they can be safely reached.

Carmarthen Fan from the Standing Stone

(overleaf)

Known also as the 'Lost' mountain, it escaped my attention for years as its name did not appear on the maps. Nevertheless, as it is the highest peak in south-western Wales it deserves some mention in these pages, and it is observed to advantage from the Standing Stone above the A4067, an old road running beside the River Tawe to Trecastle.

The summit of Fan Hir

It is nearly four miles from the nearest road to the summit of this mountain if the ascent is made by the long ridge, which displays its rosy appearance to perfection in this photograph.

Fan Foel from Llyn y Fan Fawr

(overleaf)

Lying beneath the summit of Carmarthen Fan, this lake is well placed to provide the walker with a short rest after crossing the rising moor. To the left of it, and out of this picture, rises the Staircase which, at a break in the cliffs, gives easy access to Bannau Brycheiniog, the strangely named summit.

Bannau Sir Gaer

This sheer eminence of fine elevation is the
most remarkable feature of the mountain, whose
steep, riven façade and horizontal strata will
catch the eye of the passing climber.

Llyn y Fan Fach

(overleaf)

Reaching the summit of Bannau Sir Gaer, the walker sees below the last cwm, cradling the second lake. The path leads on to Llanddeusant, but unless a car awaits the walker there, he would be well advised to retrace his steps, with an easy descent across the moor.

The Brecon Beacons

These hills are seen at their best from the lofty golf-course to the north of Brecon. They form a compact and shapely group between the Black Mountains and Carmarthen Fan. Pen y Fan is the highest peak in the group and also in South Wales, dominating this beautiful National Park. All of it is fine walking country in clear weather, but in mist the Brecon Beacons' precipitous flanks can be dangerous and are best left alone.

Pen y Fan from Bryn Teg

(overleaf)

The riven precipices of this peak, seen at their best by morning light, increase in magnificence during the ascent of this steep rib. The summit cairn may be most easily reached from the Storey Arms on the A470, but this approach lacks the visual drama of the climb from Bailea, a farm some three miles to the south of Brecon.

A remnant of Llanthony Priory

The ruins of this twelfth-century priory of Augustine canons are fairly extensive, the magnificent walls and arches still standing in places to their full height. They grace the Vale of Ewas, the longest and most beautiful valley penetrating the fastnesses of the Black Mountains, whose three whaleback ridges cover an area of some eighty square miles to the north of Abergavenny. They are dominated by the Gadair Ridge which is crowned by Waun Fach. The whole of this area is splendid walking country.

John's Arch

This strange structure spans the B4574 a short distance from the Devil's Bridge, and according to a plaque on the Arch it was erected in 1810 by Thomas Johnnes Esquire of Hafod to mark the golden jubilee of George III's accession to the throne. There is a picnic site nearby, in Myherin Forest.

Plynlimon and Duffryn Castell
(overleaf)

This is the starting point for the longer ascent of Plynlimon, where the path rises across the hillside seen in this photograph. A shorter ascent begins at Eisteddfa Gurig and keeps to an old mine-track, finally crossing the boggy moorland by a line of stakes which leads to the summit cairn.

The Bird Rock

Known also as Craig Aderyn, this striking
eminence is conspicuous from the road to the
north of Towyn, and may also be reached by
road six miles to the south-west of Tal-y-Llyn.
The Rock is appropriately named, being the
haunt of innumerable birds among which the
hawk and the cormorant are common. It is one
of the few inland breeding-places of the latter.

Tal-y-Llyn

(overleaf)

This charming lake lies at the head of a narrow valley in one of the most beautiful situations in Wales. The adjoining hotel is patronized by anglers – not just by the ordinary fisherman always hoping to catch a better basket somewhere else, but by the connoisseur of fly-casting and spinning, who returns regularly to this haunt of the wily brown trout.

The approach to Cwm y Cau

Tal-y-Llyn is conveniently situated for the most interesting ascent of Cadair Idris, whose rugged spurs can be seen beyond the lake. The walk can be undertaken by anyone who is fit and the first impressive scene of many is the approach to Cwm y Cau, as seen in this photograph. Here the rocky valley is dominated by the peak of Craig y Cau, but the small lake hidden at its base is not disclosed until its shore is reached.

The finest view of the Cwm

(overleaf)

The finest view of this wild scene is revealed by climbing the slopes on the right of the valley, where the tarn is then seen to lie at the very foot of the precipices of Craig y Cau.

Cyfrwy

The above-named spur rises to the west of Pen y Gadair and is supported by a shattered rock ridge that involves a dangerous climb. Its chief merit is that it unveils all the hills to the north: on a clear day Snowdon can be picked out above and beyond the ridges of the Harlech Dome.

Pen y Gadair

(overleaf)

Cyfrwy also yields the finest view of the summit of Cadair Idris, below which (and out of this picture) falls the long scree slope of the notorious Foxes Path.

Aran Fawddwy from Drysgol

The lofty Arans are excellent walking country, and their two summits crown the highest ridge south of Snowdonia. They are best approached from Dinas Mawddwy by way of the hamlet of Aber Cywarch, where the narrow road ends at a footbridge giving access to an old peat track. This rises gently across the hillside for two miles and emerges at the best viewpoint in the group – Drysgol – at a height of 2,000 feet. This is the small tarn seen in this picture; beyond it the distant ridge rises gradually to Aran Fawddwy.

Aran Benllyn and Creiglyn Dyfi

(overleaf)

From the last belvedere, the view to the right opens up a fine mountain scene dominated by Aran Benllyn (only 69 feet lower than its peer, Aran Fawddwy). The small tarn cupped in the hillside is the remote and lonely birthplace of the famous River Dovey.

The Moelwyns

The Afon Glaslyn is a good viewpoint for the appraisal of this mountain whose three peaks make a pleasant traverse on a sunny morning. They are usually climbed from the isolated hamlet of Croesor, seen in the next picture.

Croesor

This hamlet is also the key to the easy ascent of
Cnicht, the most interesting mountain in this
area because it reveals a comprehensive
panorama of the whole of Snowdonia. The
skyline in this photograph is dominated by
Moel Hebog on the left and by the Nantlle
Ridge on the right.

Cnicht from Tan-Lan

(overleaf)

This view of the 'Matterhorn of Wales' with its attractive, colourful foreground was taken from a bridge spanning the stream nearby.

The Glaslyn River

Autumn turns the bracken to gold on the banks
of this peaceful river – a popular viewpoint
from the layby opposite.

Aberglaslyn Pass

(overleaf)

This well known and well loved scene also
looks its most beautiful in late autumn.

Beddgelert

This picturesque village is not only the key to the southern approaches to Snowdonia, but is also famous for Gelert's Grave, a cairn in a meadow near the church, said to mark the grave of the faithful hound in the ancient fable. Beddgelert's hotels and cottages on the banks of the Glaslyn River stand at the junction of three lovely valleys, each of which is well worth a visit.

The Nantlle Ridge from Beddgelert

(overleaf)

Rising on the western fringes of Snowdonia, this lofty ridge is one of the most beautiful in the region but is generally known only to the connoisseur.

Y Garn II and Mynydd Mawr from Llyn y Gadair

These two peaks guard the entrance to Drwy-y-Coed Pass, and that on the left marks the beginning of the Nantlle Ridge.

Snowdon from the summit of Y Garn II

(overleaf)

On attaining the summit of this hill, Snowdon bursts upon the view, as seen in this picture.

Mynydd Mawr from the Summit

This peak, rising due north of Y Garn II, is
fronted by the shattered crags of Craig y Bere
which, however, are so unstable that they are
seldom visited by the climber.

Llyn Nantlle Uchaf

(overleaf)

I have seen this lovely lake in a variety of moods, ruffled with wind and white horses, or shining like a mirror. But it looks its best on a tranquil autumn afternoon, with Snowdon looming in the gap between Craig y Bere on the left and Y Garn II on the right.

The Great Slab in Cwmsilin

The immense vertical rock-face seen in this
picture draws many a climber to tackle its 400
feet of difficult ascent.

Mynydd Mawr from Llyn y Dywarchan

(overleaf)

This beautiful sheet of water, one of the most colourful foregrounds for a photograph of Mynydd Mawr, is now open only to fishermen.

Craig Cwm-bychan and Llyn Cwellyn

The Snowdon Ranger is possibly the first known
route to the summit of the dominating peak of
Wales, and this is one of the many photographs
that can be successfully taken from it.

Llyn D'ur Arddu

(overleaf)

This picture was also taken from the upper stretches of the Snowdon Ranger – the sudden revelation of the rock-bound tarn far below is sensational. It lies at the foot of the most important climbing crag in all Snowdonia.

Snowdon from the south

(overleaf pp 80/81)

A spacious prospect of the upper section of the popular Rhyd-ddu path to Snowdon: it is one of the easiest and most interesting ascents of the peak.

Bwlch Main

This is the final section of the Rhyd-ddu route to Snowdon. Despite its seeming exposure and steepness, it is quite safe if care is taken.

Moel Siabod

(overleaf)

Many visitors to Snowdonia enter this beautiful National Park at Betws-y-Coed, and the first mountain to catch the eye when near the Ugly House is this graceful peak, overlooking the village of Capel Curig.

The approach to Moel Siabod

Those who ascend Moel Siabod by way of the
bridge spanning Cyfyng Falls soon attain a
grassy cart-track with views ahead of their peak.
And in the autumn they may be fortunate
enough to meet the shepherd bringing down his
flock for winter grazing.

The Cliffs of
Moel Siabod

(overleaf)

Llyn y Foel lies at the foot of this mountain's eastern flanks, whose precipitous rock-face may come as a surprise to the walker. The rocky ridge in the background of this photograph must be climbed to attain the cairn on the summit of Moel Siabod, which opens up a splendid panorama of Snowdon.

The Pinnacles of Capel Curig

Frowning upon the little village, these rocky
pinnacles are easily reached by a short walk
from the Post Office and reveal excellent views
of the enclosing hills.

A splendid prospect of Snowdon

(overleaf)

The eye is first attracted by the white walls of Plas y Brenin, the National Mountaineering Centre, and then skims across the blue of the Llynnau Mymbyr, to rest finally upon the majestic Snowdon group of mountains.

Teaching a student to abseil

The slab-like rocks of the Pinnacles are well placed for Plas y Brenin, and students there can receive expert tuition in this essential technique of the mountaineer.

A Golden Carneddau

(overleaf)

This unusually beautiful picture was taken from these pinnacles on a wonderful autumn morning, and reveals some of the well known peaks in northern Snowdonia.

The Afon Llugwy

(overleaf pp 98/99)

Rising in the Carneddau beneath the crowning peak of Carnedd Llywelyn, the river takes a twisting course on its way to Capel Curig, and makes an alternative foreground for many shots of the encircling hills.

Helyg – The Climbers' Club Hut

Well known to the mountaineering fraternity,
this Hut is splendidly situated for the ascent of
the three great buttresses of Tryfan.

Tryfan from the Hut

In springtime this austere landscape is
transformed by the beauty of fresh green leaves
on the trees near the Hut.

The changing tapestry of autumn

(overleaf)

Later in the year, this same scene is painted by Nature in scarlet and gold.

Llyn Ogwen

Enclosed by a fine circuit of hills, this well
known lake lies at the head of Nant Ffrancon
and is dominated by Y Garn, seen on the left of
the picture.

Ogwen Falls

(overleaf)

These turbulent falls, near the road below Ogwen Cottage, are a remarkable sight when in spate. Also of considerable interest, though unknown to many visitors, is the fact that beneath the arch of the bridge on the left is the original bridge, possibly built by the Romans.

Pen Llithrig-y-Wrach

Seen from Capel Curig, this shapely peak
dominates the vast moorland and overlooks
Llyn Cowlyd. Stakes driven into the ground
indicate an approach route which avoids
stretches of bog in wet weather.

Carnedd Llywelyn from Ffynnon Llugwy

(overleaf)

There are two interesting routes to this lofty peak which crowns the immense Carneddau. This one leaves the Holyhead road near Helyg, and in its higher reaches passes Craig yr Ysfa, a favourite playground of the rock climber.

Craig yr Ysfa

Seen from the adjacent ridge of Pen yr Helig-
du, the precipitous northern front of Craig yr
Ysfa soars up at the head of Cwm Eigau.

A climber on the Amphitheatre Buttress

The path to Carnedd Llywelyn passes along the edge of a vast natural amphitheatre, with this breath-takingly sheer buttress on its western flank.

The Synchant Pass

(overleaf)

This is one of the memorable surprises in store for the driver who starts his tour from Conwy, and is bound for Penmaenmar – the sudden appearance of an enchanting valley backed by the glittering sea.

The Buttresses of Tryfan

One of the shapeliest peaks in Snowdonia,
Tryfan is suddenly revealed on the eastern
approach to Nant Ffrancon. Its three
magnificent buttresses are the special preserve of
the rock climber.

A pool reflection on Bwlch Caseg-fraith

(overleaf)

The walker who ascends the eastern rim of Cwm Tryfan will not only have a spectacular view of the mountain, but on a calm day will also delight in its perfect reflection in the pools lying on this lofty watershed.

A stormy day by the pool

(overleaf pp 124/125)

While wandering up to the Glyders on a dark wild day, hoping for some light so that I could use my Leica, I suddenly saw a break in the fast-moving clouds. The sun came through like a searchlight, and just as it passed overhead I released the shutter on my camera – resulting in the picture shown here. It was the only shot I took that day, but was a rare prize for any landscape photographer.

The Milestone Buttress

This well known crag stands high above the
tenth milestone from Bangor, quite near Ogwen
Cottage. It is a very popular training ground
for enthusiastic rock climbers.

This rocky ridge, which involves some
scrambling, rewards mountain walkers with
magnificent views of hill and lake to the west.

The summit of Tryfan

(overleaf)

After the arduous ascent of the North Ridge,
this summit is a favourite resting place for all
climbers, and on a clear day it opens up a
marvellous panorama of the surrounding hills.
This shot was taken from the southern slopes
of the peak.

Adam and Eve

These two vertical boulders, known as Adam and Eve, crown Tryfan, and they are both clearly revealed against the sky on the approach from Capel Curig. It is difficult enough to attain the top of one of them – it requires a very steady head to step from one to the other.

Bristly Ridge

(overleaf)

Seen at its finest from Bwlch Caseg-fraith, this seemingly difficult pinnacled ridge is in fact only a good scramble, and is a popular route to Glyder Fach.

The Cantilever

Situated near the top of Bristly Ridge, this
horizontal slab has given rise to the question as
to how many people it will support. Rumour
has it that over twenty schoolboys were once
seen on it without any tilt of the slab!

Glyder Fach

An enormous collection of great slabs and
boulders, this summit gives many a young
scrambler the opportunity to test his skill.

The Castle of the Winds

(overleaf)

Castell y Gwynt appears as an obstacle in the traverse of the Glyders, and care must be taken during the descent of its western side which consists largely of vertical masses of slate.

Llyn Idwal

This beautiful sheet of water, cradled in a
magnificent rocky cwm, is easily reached from
Ogwen Cottage by a well-paved path. Many
romantic Welsh legends are associated with it.

Idwal Slabs

(overleaf)

Legions of rock climbers are attracted by these famous sloping crags, which at first sight appear to offer easy routes of ascent. But when tackled, these three courses alone – known as Faith, Hope and Charity – are much more difficult than they appear. None of the innumerable courses on these slabs is easy.

The Devil's Kitchen

(overleaf p 145)

This precipitous gap, which forms a conspicuous break in the skyline of the Glyders as seen from Llyn Idwal, should be left severely alone by all walkers. Its difficult ascent is strictly the preserve of the experienced rock climber.

Cwm Idwal from Pen yr Ole Wen

Reaching the summit of this Carneddau peak
involves some rough going, but its rewards are
immense – it reveals the whole of Cwm Idwal
to perfection on a sunny summer afternoon.

Snowdon from the Royal Bridge

(overleaf)

Foreground is a most important feature of a good photograph, and in this one (taken with a 90 mm lens) the bridge satisfies the eye, backed as it is by the whole Snowdon group.

A wintry view of the group

Snow enhances the appearance of most
mountains, and of none more than Snowdon –
the highest peak south of the Border.

Pen-y-Gwryd

(overleaf)

Perhaps the most famous climbers' centre in the whole of Snowdonia, this hotel stands at the junction of the roads to Llanberis and Beddgelert. It has a long mountaineering history and will always be closely associated with the Climbers' and Pinnacle Clubs, formed here in relatively recent years. It was at this hotel also that the first mountaineers stayed in Snowdonia. They came here because of its easy access to Snowdon and its near neighbour Lliwedd, whose cliffs were first explored in detail at the turn of the century.

Snowdon and Crib Goch from Nantgwynant

The car-park is well situated for this splendid
mountain view, and is very popular with
tourists.

A quiet morning by Llyn Gwynant

(overleaf)

Possibly the most beautiful lake in Snowdonia, Llyn Gwynant can often be seen like this early in the day, before the wind ruffles its surface. It is the finest viewpoint for Yr Aran.

The Glyders from Llyn Gwynant

An autumn view from the same lake, when the colours were at their best.

Moel Hebog from Llyn Dinas

(overleaf)

Cradled in the lower stretches of Nantgwynant, this lake makes an excellent foreground for Beddgelert's own mountain.

Cnicht and the Moelwyns from Moel Hebog

The ascent of Moel Hebog involves some
strenuous walking, but the wide panorama from
its summit is worth the effort. This photograph
discloses the surprising length of Cnicht's lofty
ridge, in great contrast to the view of the peak
from Tan-Lan.

Caernarfon

(overleaf)

A good camera-study of this famous city
depends on conditions of light and stillness,
such as existed when this shot was taken. The
red lamp on the boat in the foreground
contributes much to the picture's charm.

Snowdon from the Eagle Tower

(overleaf pp 166/167)

Those who have climbed the endless steps to
this high vantage-point in Caernarfon Castle
deserve a rewarding view, but they will only be
able to see the distant mountains on a clear day.

Snowdon from Llyn Padarn

Water in the foreground of any photograph
usually enhances its appeal. This shot was taken
from the northern shore of the lake, with the
added interest of autumn colours along its
shore.

Llanberis Pass from Dolbadarn Castle

(overleaf)

Looking *down* the Pass shows the long line of
cliffs enclosing it, with lakes in the far distance
(see pp 180/181); but looking *up* is usually of less
interest. However in this picture the Castle leads
the eye along the slopes of Snowdon to the
ridge of Crib Goch.

One of the famous boulders

This boulder is one of three lying beside the road in the Llanberis Pass which were threatened with demolition for a road-widening scheme. My friend Harvey Lloyd (in the picture) saw holes being drilled for blasting, and started a campaign which, after nearly six years, resulted in their reprieve.

Dinas y Gromlech

(overleaf)

These spectacular cliffs rise above the boulders in the Pass and attract the toughest members of our climbing fraternity. Cemetery Gates, one of the hardest courses, was first climbed by Joe Brown and Don Whillans.

Pen y Pass in my early days

Years ago the Gorphwysfa Hotel stood in splendid isolation at the top of the Pass. The distinguished mountaineer, Geoffrey Winthrop Young, author of *Mountaineering Craft*, the then accepted work on mountaineering techniques, often stayed here: he will be remembered by many for the annual Easter parties he gave, mainly to university students.

Pen y Pass today

(overleaf)

The hotel was later transformed into one of the finest youth hostels in the country, and there is now a restaurant nearby. This is the favoured starting point for the ascent of the Snowdon Horseshoe and for other routes to Yr Yddfa.

Looking down the Llanberis Pass

One of the most famous passes in Snowdonia, it
winds its way down to Nant Peris, enclosed by
stupendous cliffs.

Crib Goch from Pen y Pass

(overleaf)

Seen at its finest from the doors of the youth hostel, this rocky peak is the first one to be climbed in the traverse of the Horseshoe.

The last Nail in the Horseshoe

This isolated rock, standing high above Pen y
Pass, derived its name from its remarkable
shape – like that of an immense nail.

The Horseshoe
from Crib Goch

(overleaf)

Before midday Crib Goch is the finest
viewpoint for photographs of the whole of the
curving ridge. But if left until later, much of
the ridge then appears in silhouette, losing all
the detail that is so important to the climber.

Crossing the narrow ridge

Exposed ridges such as this one require special care and balance from any mountaineer: in my early days the test was to walk across it with one's hands behind one's head!

Crib Goch from Cwm Glas

(overleaf)

The ridge on the skyline is seen at its best from this remote and lonely cwm.

Snowdon summit from Carnedd Ugain

On attaining Carnedd Ugain by the well-worn
track on the Horseshoe, Snowdon is near at
hand and is reached by following the skyline to
the left, where the path runs beside the railway
almost up to the summit cairn. There is a
glimpse of Lliwedd on the left of this picture.

Lliwedd from Snowdon

(overleaf)

The fabulous panorama disclosed from this dominating peak includes most of the hills in the National Park: this photograph shows only part of the view – the continuation of the Horseshoe.

Close-up of the east peak of Lliwedd

On reaching the west peak of Lliwedd by a
narrow and sensational track on the very edge
of the cliffs overlooking Llyn Llydaw, its
neighbour, the east peak, is seen to advantage,
with its rocky precipices dropping away into
space.

The cliffs of Lliwedd from below

The almost vertical cliffs of this peak are seen at their best during the descent to Llyn Llydaw. As noted in the caption on p 151, they attracted many well known mountaineers who, at the turn of the century, were independent gentlemen from the universities and the professions. It was they who explored this crag in detail and named many of the courses.

In later years, however, the sport of rock climbing attracted our athletic youth, and the subsequent exploration of almost every crag in Wales is due to their enthusiasm.

Snowdon from Llyn Llydaw

(overleaf)

This is the classic view of the dramatic eastern front of Yr Yddfa (the Welsh name for Snowdon), but to make a satisfactory picture of it the tarn must be full of water. Otherwise the lateral moraines mar the wonderful beauty of the scene.

Moel Siabod from Llyn Teryn

On the return walk to Pen y Pass, the track
passes above this tarn, where the derelict
buildings were at one time occupied by miners.

Canoes on the Capel lakes

(overleaf)

These lakes are near enough to Plas y Brenin to allow its students of climbing and mountain walking to enjoy canoeing as well.

Sunset from the same viewpoint

(overleaf pp 206/207)

I have seen more dramatically beautiful sunsets from the Llynnau Mymbyr than from any other place in Britain. This one was taken with an exposure of 1/60 of a second at F4 on Kodachrome 25 which, in similar atmospheric conditions, yields the most beautiful transparencies.